STUFF (FIRST-TIME) AUTHORS NEED TO KNOW...

11 Steps to create your (super) book

By Amy R Brooks

*This book is dedicated to all the authors
who need a little love before they bare their stories.*

This book is your hug; your hand to hold.

*Be brave, be scared, be excited…
be an author.*

TABLE OF CONTENTS

❖

PREFACE

❖

I am a writer. I am an author.

Most people I've met do not like to declare these titles. They want to daydream about them and put them on a bucket list, but they do not want to claim them for themselves. Yet.

Deciding to become an author, and owning that space, feels too lofty for many casual writers. I hear countless folks talk about their journaling, blogging, articles, and even book drafts with an over-reaching humility that requires a lot of self-examination.

What does it mean to be a writer or an author that so many of us shrink down and step aside? I have one theory that may apply to most shy-story-tellers: we have so much respect for published authors and their craft that we don't want to soil the field with our silly writing projects.

I have news for you my friend. There are LOADS of books out there that are not necessarily amazing and would not appeal to you as a buyer. Those writers/authors are still reaching out to their audience. They're still sharing their insights through the written word. The books that *you* may not respect (and fear being lumped together with) are still impacting the world. Those writers are a part of a larger conversation; one that is written, in print, and ongoing.

Creating books is not like making a Facebook comment or a blog post. Writing a book is a project that results in a permanent product that can live on with more stamina than a passing blurb on social media. While it doesn't have to be perfect, you will give it much more attention than that early morning post. Your book will be read, and re-read, revised, edited, and rewritten. It will have a polish that you rarely extend to other writings. Your book will be permanent and polished.

But things change and this one permanent and polished book will not define you for all times.

The book you write over the next 3-6 months will be a reflection of you and your perspective at this particular time. A book you write in 5 years from now will reflect your perspective at that time. You will change, your views will change, and your writing will change. A book is merely a fluid moment in time captured in a permanent collection of pages that can be shared by members of your tribe around the world.

It's a big deal and it's not a big deal.

It's amazing to think that you can share your wisdom with others. *You* can speak your truth in an authentic, polished, organized way. It won't be rushed, you won't have typos, you won't have to scurry to find the perfect meme to accompany your words. Your book will be carefully groomed and sculpted over time until you are ready to share it. People may read your book and feel heard and represented by you and your words. That's cool. It's kind of a big deal; which can make it feel a little heavy and intimidating.

It's also amazing to think about how many books are written that you will never read in this lifetime. There are *millions* of books that have been written that you will never read! Your book many not end up being that big of a deal. There are so many books, that no one knows how many books actually exist on our planet! It's kind of like the number of stars in the sky or sand on the beach;

there are just too many to count. Your sweet book may be in the mix and enjoyed by a portion of readers, but it won't be read by everyone. You will have eyes on your book, but it's probably not going to be read by anyone outside your tribe.

Your tribe, by the way, is the distinct group of people you attract to yourself when you share your message. You probably have a following online, and many of those casual connections may end up in your tribe once you declare your specific niche. Maybe you've already established your brand or message and you know who is digging it and down for the cause. Great! They will be the ones who buy your book. Then they'll actually read it and share it with their friends and colleagues. They will help you market your book and attract new members to your tribe.

So what's the main message of this preface? Write your book and they will come.

Moving forward, let's simply acknowledge that you're going to be an author. It doesn't matter if that title doesn't feel like a natural fit right now. You'll have time to grow into it over the next few months; your perspective will grow as your book grows. Pretty soon a lot of things will shift for you- books do that to you! This book is your guide on the side as you navigate the steps of writing your book: from deciding on an audience to developing your voice and message. We'll also cover the side projects you'll need to start *while* working on your draft. Oh, and we will definitely be working on your author authority. You're going to claim it with grace and confidence by the time we finish this process.

No more intro...let's get started!

"I am a writer.
I am an author." - You

STEP 1

❖

YOU'RE CONSTIPATED.

I really like analogies and, unfortunately, I really like the feeling behind this chapter title and subsequent analogy.

Sorry, not sorry.

When you're constipated you really want relief. You feel backed up, full, and uncomfortable. Ahh, same feeling you get when you have a story that is needs to be told! You have a feeling of urgency and discomfort that you're not quite sure what to do with.

Good! You're constipated with a story and you want to get it OUT! It's scary to feel like you have something you want to get out; especially if you are afraid you will meet resistance. Maybe you're feeling resistance from yourself or from others, but you definitely have a sense that this story-writing process is not going to be smooth sailing. On some soulful level you can tell that if writing a book was so easy, then a lot more folks would have done it by now.

It must be hard, painful, unpleasant…some kind of terrible!

But that fear coexists with a throbbing sense of importance. You realize that your book may be important…to someone, somewhere, at some point in the future. You're not completely sure of this fact, but you wonder if it could become important once it's written. Then you worry that if you continue to procrastinate, you might find yourself in a lot more pain than you currently feel.

You question yourself further: Could you actually be in more discomfort than you currently feel? How would it feel to let yourself down on such a deep level? What if this is one of the more important acts you are meant to take in your lifetime… and you don't do it?

Yikes! All of this worrying is going to take you in a rapid spiral of drama that I'm not interested in watching. Let's switch gears: instead of wondering or worrying, let's ponder the possibilities.

If you sit down and write a little here and a little there, you may have a better idea of what all this constipation is about. By simply acknowledging your urges and relaxing about the future, you may be able to get a handle on what you being called to do as a writer.

Assuming that you have an urge to write a book for teen girls who are going through depression, you might sit down and start to journal about why you *must* write this book. In your relaxed state of acceptance, you may discover a sense of relief as you write and you find that sharing your experiences using pen and paper has a different feel to it than when you simply talk or think about depression. You may notice that the words flow to you and you cannot stop writing. You suddenly remember things about your friends who were there for you when your parents didn't understand your muted distance from them.

Maybe you start writing about the friend who lost their battle with depression and committed suicide. You're surprised that writing about that loss makes it hurt less, not more. Eventually your hand starts to cramp and you look at the pages filled with your buried thoughts, feelings, stories, and lessons. You are a bit surprised that you had more information backed up within you than you even realized. You have let it out. You didn't mean to; you'd been holding onto those stories and emotions for so long that you feel adrift now.

Did you really write out the details of the day you stayed in bed and cried for 5 straight hours?! How did that story come out of you? Where was that story? You'd almost forgotten about it and now it's here, written on the page in front of you. Yes, the story is only two to three sentences long at this point, but you captured the feelings behind the tears that day. You referenced the weakness you felt when the headaches came and the dehydration set in. You will be able to revisit that moment in time later, but for now it has been heard, recognized, respected, and recorded. That memory is satisfied with you and will now rest comfortably on the page instead of the deep, cramped recesses of your long-term memory. It will no longer clog your joy with its residual shame.

Yes, you wrote more in your journal, but this

story means so much because you didn't even re-member it was there. You knew parts of you felt bad and you wanted freedom, but you weren't sure what parts were exactly pushing against your sub-conscious for recognition. Now you know. Now you can see, on the page before you, which parts of your history were grieving you. They were making you feel uncomfortable long after you had forgot-ten that they even existed.

So then you sleep, and dream lightly.

You write some more.

You don't try to write a book, but you do give yourself permission to write out what you think you should write a book about.

You want to see what you're working with. Is it any good? What memories are actually available to share with others?

And your constipation, all that pressure, starts to lessen. You can feel the healing that comes with relaxing and resting. You exhale as you write and release your thoughts. And then you laugh at how messy it is on the page. With a smile, you look over each sheet of paper.

Here's a thought you started and then abandoned (not a big deal, you know how it ends) and over here is a list of names you must have suddenly remembered. You start recounting all of the teachers you had and who did what for you, or to you, during the lowest points of your depression. Amazing details that you could only unearth after you had written the previous information. You are an archeologist of memories; your valuable assets are buried deep under your subconscious and need to be discovered. These memories have lessons and wisdom and they are beautiful. They shine brightly on the page; so grateful that someone has found them.

<u>Action Step:</u> Writing to Understand

Could you actually be in more discomfort than you currently feel?

_____

_____

_____

_____

_____

_____

_____

How would it feel to let yourself down on such a deep level?

_____

_____

_____

_____

_____

_____

_____

What if this is one of the more important acts you are meant to take in your lifetime…and you don't do it?

_____

_____

_____

_____

_____

_____

_____

_____

Start listing all of the things you could write about below. No judgment. Just write:

_____

_____

_____

_____

_____

_____

_____

_____

*"You exhale as you write and
release your thoughts.
And then you laugh at how messy
it is on the page."*

And now you're a writer! You have stopped trying to fight your constipation. You have gotten out of your head and gotten in flow with your stories. Instead of blocking them with worry and logic, you stepped aside and said "come out if you want to" and, boy, did they want to come out!

This is a messy affair. Writing may bring back tears and emotions even if you're not writing about teen depression. You may get swept up in a story about love or loss. I cry tears of gratitude when I think about all of my blessings. Folks get emotional when they tell triumphant stories of overcoming obstacles or tragic tales about losing it all.

It is inevitable that we are going to get emotional as we welcome the ideas and stories that come rushing forth. Those stories come carrying luggage full of details. We don't have to empty the luggage just yet, but we get emotional because we know how overstuffed those bags may be. We have a keen understanding that those bags will be opened and when they are, things are going to get intense.

And so now you have less pressure.

But y ou did not write a book.

You wrote a bunch of scribbly stuff in your journal. You feel better, but you also realize why you felt bad in the first place. Holding in thoughts and emotions can be exhausting, especially when you tell yourself that you have no other choice but to hold them in.

Well, now you have a choice.

You can continue to feel good and write on. You can find deeper, long-lasting relief by taking the next step. You were not meant to simply journal and then die. You are taking the first step to prepare for your path of authorship.

Releasing your story ideas was a great first step towards writing a book, but it's not enough. The path before you winks in recognition. It knows you are going to travel down it and learn about yourself along the way. It is ready for you. This path will guide you to your audience. They are waiting and they are ready to receive the stories and emotions you are preparing for them.

Take the next step for you...and your future readers.

"Releasing your story ideas was a great first step towards writing a book, but it's not enough."

(one more) Action Step:

Imagine your future reader...then write a brief letter to them. Tell them **why** you want to "talk" to them.

_____

_____

_____

_____

_____

_____

_____

_____

_____

_____

_____

_____

STEP 2

— ❖ —

FEEL BETTER.

Ah, the sweet relief of release. I won't overdo it with the constipation metaphor, but there is something to be said about releasing something we have held onto for too long. If you're nervous, scared, worried, or annoyed at the thought of writing, then you are holding on. You tell yourself that you're too busy or not talented, but that icky feeling that comes with those excuses is emanating from the tight grip you have on your fear. It's time to admit that you're holding onto a hypothetical fear of failure when it comes to writing.

I'm going to use another analogy (with less bowel-based imagery) to demonstrate how this particular fear might show up for you. When you think about writing, or any activity that seems intimidating, it's easy to put it in a box and put it away for a bit. It's tidy, stored, and not thrown away. It's off to the side and visible if you want to look at it for reassurance that it hasn't left. And holy shit, don't let someone tell you that you should open the box and deal with what is inside. That is *your* box and you will do with it as you please when you are good and goddamn ready!

Potential writers can get pretty snippy about their box of ideas. They know they haven't taken the time to nurture the ideas; no organizing or grappling, no coaxing or attention, but that is not the reason why the book hasn't been written. The reason the book hasn't been written is because they are too busy with their career or their housework. The book hasn't been started because they don't know what they want to say about a topic they feel passionately about. They may have another book idea that could be better. There isn't a good title for the book. Someone else has probably already written the book. The book will have errors and everyone who reads it will fixate on the mistakes. There isn't an agent or publishing house lined up. The book is too complicated to write. The book is not a daily priority, but (wait for it) it's super important and must be written.

I've lovingly listened to excuses from every writer I've ever worked with. Smart, organized women and men who are successful in most aspects of their lives can be derailed by the act of writing a book. They have wonderful intentions, but don't know how to move past the excitement of releasing ideas to actually writing the letters that become words that become sentences that become paragraphs that become chapters that become a book. Excuses choke off their genius and hide their literary expression. It's hard to watch, but it's almost inevitable.

If excuses and procrastination are predictable, dare I even say normal, then what can be done to actually progress in your writing?

Personally I need fear and goodies. Some may say carrots (rewards for accomplishment) and sticks (punishment for failure), but I'm sticking with my dueling motivators. For me, fear is real. I get afraid of letting others down. Naturally, if I work by myself on a book I won't have anyone to let down so

I've learned to ask others to expect updates from me. With this structure in place, if I don't produce those updates, I will let others down and I will feel like poopy. It may be a paying client or a writing group I'm leading, but if someone is looking to me to show up and deliver, I am terrified at the idea of letting them down. No question, I will sit my butt down and write to make sure that doesn't happen.

Conversely, I really like getting stuff I want. If I know that I can get a creamy cup of coffee, a walk around the neighborhood, a snuggle session with my husband, or a peek at Facebook after I write for an hour, I'm going to write. Combining my fears *with* some goodies is a winning combination for me. You're not me, but most of us respond to deadlines and incentives. Try it. You may be surprised how easily you can trick yourself into getting to work on those letters, words, and sentences.

After building a framework that gets you motivated to work, the most important step is to get to the keyboard. Get typing. Once you start you may be pleasantly surprised. Like, "Oh snap, I like this!"

Writing your book can be as energizing and fun as hanging out with a friend. Yes, it's a pain to change out of stinky sweats, shower, drive across town in a storm, find parking and wait for a table, but once your seated in a cozy booth with your bestie, you have a blast. It can be that way with your book- I swear! You can sit down and write for a few minutes and feel clunky and awkward, but once you find your flow and you can talk to your audience in the same way you talk to a buddy, it becomes a pleasure. This phenomenon is not that surprising when you think about the energetic exchange that is going on while you're writing. You are channeling stories, ideas, and expression creatively and things that did not previously exist have now materialized on the page. You are a creator and your creation is exactly what you want it to be. You are god. You are in complete control. It's pretty thrilling if you can loosen up and ride that wave.

At some point in this process, you're going to feel better.

Don't you want to feel better?

So make a date with your writing. Sit down and handwrite or type every possible title you'd love to use. Make-up a review someone could post after reading your book. Jot down 5 things you really, really want your audience to learn or feel once they've finished your book. Just have fun and enjoy getting to know your book a little better each time you get together.

Remember: you are the creator, so create something you enjoy coming back to again and again.

"If excuses and procrastination are predictable, dare I even say normal, then what can be done to actually progress in your writing?"

<u>Action Steps</u>: To help you bust through excuses and procrastination

Let's start with 5 possible titles you'd love to use:

_____

_____

_____

_____

_____

_____

_____

_____

Make-up a review someone could post after reading your book (make it a POSITIVE review, please):

_____

_____

_____

_____

_____

_____

_____

_____

Jot down 5 things you really, really want your audience to learn once they've finished your book:

_____

_____

_____

_____

_____

_____

_____

_____

Remember: "Writing your book can be as energizing and fun as hanging out with a friend."

STEP 3

— ❖ —

WHO, WHAT, HOW.

S ome very distinctive things must be decided before you start drafting your book. Before you start typing, you need to figure out who you're talking to...specifically. When I hear authors say, "everyone" I get nervous. Quick comparison: when I'm at a party I don't talk to everyone all at once, I choose one or two people to interact with. My topic, angle, and language are all designed to specifically engage that small group of people at that moment. If I move to a different circle of people at a party, I will adjust accordingly.

When it comes to your book, try to imagine yourself talking to a group of people. Who are they? If you imagine someone like yourself, great! Your book should appeal to readers who like the same things that you like. If you're still stuck on wanting to talk to everyone, the equivalent of making a general announcement to every partygoer attending an event, then you're going to have to figure out what will appeal to everyone.

Moving forward, it would be hugely beneficial for you to mentally picture your ideal reader; really imagine the person you're talking to in your book (refer back to that letter you wrote them in the last chapter).

Once you know your WHO, sit down and describe them in a sentence or two. Here is my WHO for this book and some space for you to write your own.

My WHO for this book- *First-time authors who want to write a book; a whole book, within the next 3-6 months. The general mental/emotional age of the writers is 25-65 years old.*

Your WHO-

_____

_____

_____

What you want to say to this specific audience is critically important! Confession: I have SO much to say about almost everything, nearly all of the time. That overwhelming character trait of mine has to go on the shelf when it comes to book-writing; no need to overwhelm folks! When it comes to writing your book, you must figure out *one* message you want to share more than any other message. You need to sit down and decide which take-aways are most valuable to your reader at this time. Don't stress over this, you can write other books with any discarded messages you can't stand to abandon completely. Sometimes just knowing that you can resurrect topics in the future, helps us to focus on going deeper within the book in front of us now. Now what...

Your WHAT is going to tell your audience if your book is going to fill a need they have in their life. If they feel like your message is one they need to hear, they'll pick up the book. Customers want to know what you're offering before they pay money to read on, so don't be coy or mysterious. You may actually use the message we're about to draft for the blurb on the back cover of your book. If potential readers can't figure out what your book is going to cover, they will flip it over and read the summary on the back. That brief summary is your last chance to persuade them to give your book a chance. That summary is your WHAT; it's the main message you want to convey to readers.

Now in a sentence or two, describe WHAT you want your reader to learn by reading your book. I'll provide an example again and then you'll have space to develop your main idea as well.

My WHAT for this book- *Readers will understand why they are writing their book, they will create a sustainable routine for creating their first draft, and they will gain confidence and clarity about their writing voice.*

Your WHAT-

_____

_____

_____

_____

_____

_____

_____

Asking the HOW is my favorite because I interpret the HOW as, "How do you want your audience to feel when they're done reading your book?" We're going to go way beyond feeling good and get specific about our goals. You can write a book that gives your reader a sense of peace or a sense of dread and urgency. Some books I've read have lifted my vibe and inspired me to dream bigger. Other books have moved me to tears of outrage or gratitude. I've read books that brought up a range of emotions by the time I reached the back cover, but I generally had one overall feeling when I thought back to that reading experience.

If you're a book lover and you vary your reading material, you can probably recall the books that made you laugh, cry, shiver, worry, or swoon. Your book has the power to do that to a random person on the other side of the planet! You can write to inspire, soothe, or scare; it's totally your call.

Before you start writing, or even consider the writing schedule that will sustain you from the opening preface to the blurb on the back cover, you need to nail down HOW you want your audience to feel when they close your book cover that final time.

My HOW for this book- *Readers will feel energized and focused by the time they finish the first half of this book. By the time they get to the end they will feel empowered because they will have a (nearly?) finished manuscript of their own. Overall the readers/soon-to-be authors will feel powerful!*

Your HOW-

_____

_____

_____

_____

_____

_____

_____

_____

We will refer back to your WHO, WHAT, and HOW later on. It's important to keep reminding ourselves of our initial vision and keep a consistent focus throughout our book. For now, we are going to take one step closer to actually starting the draft of your book by deciding WHEN you're going to make time to write on a day-to-day basis.

"You can write to inspire, soothe, or scare; it's totally your call."

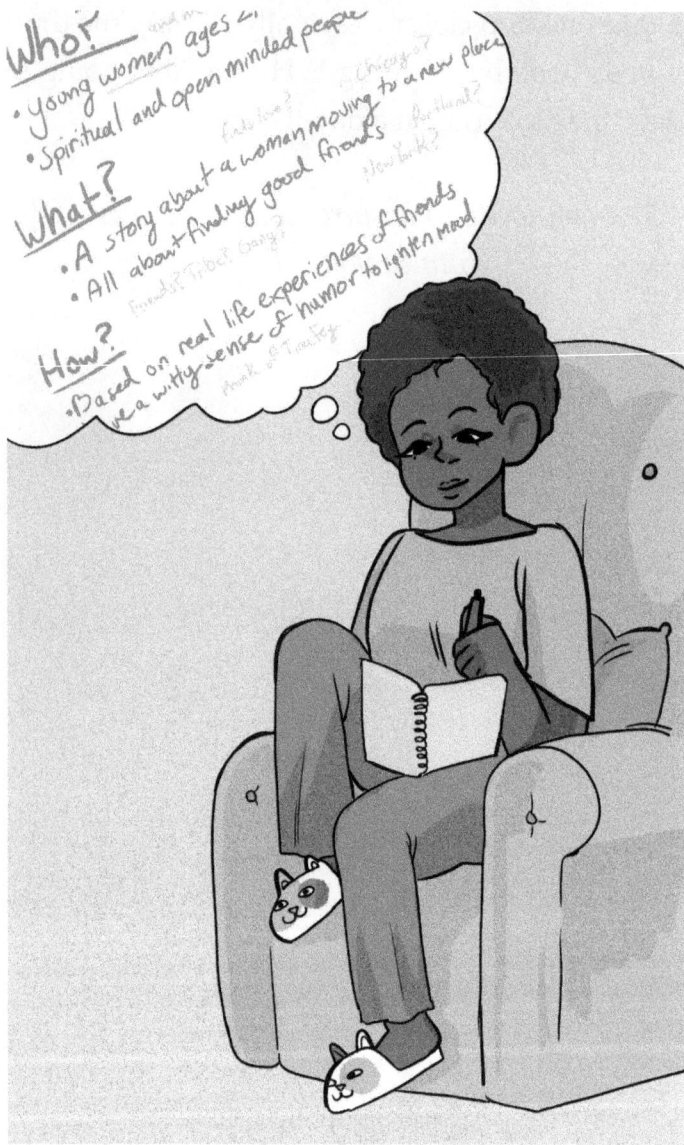

STEP 4

❖

WHATCHA GONNA SAY?

It's time to sit down and brainstorm the details of your book. I feel pretty strongly that this can be a magical experience. Your message *should* be magical. Your book can stand out from all other books on the subject if it sparkles with originality and passion.

So how do you make your message, and the process of brainstorming details, magical? With an outline, friends.

The beautiful, sexy, intriguing qualities inherent to an outline naturally lend themselves to a mystical endeavor.

Just kidding.

Usually outlining can be dull and overly-systematic. I would like to change that stereotype for you. I want you to fall in love with the power of your outline to communicate your message in a way that surprises and delights you. You outline is going to be your buddy who remembers all of the nitty-gritty parts of your story. When you sit in front of a blank screen on the computer and feel a wave of panic rising in your stomach on its way to your chest, simply turn to your trusty outline and find peace. As you look over the topics and subtopics of your outline, you'll suddenly remember all of the great aspects you dreamed up for that particular chapter. You'll see that you had a special anecdote in mind for a tricky concept. You'll read how you thought a quick brainstorming activity will help your reader get started.

By the time you're done re-reading the notes that you took days, weeks, or months earlier, you will feel focused and inspired all over again. Outlines are your buddy. They want to help you when you're feeling adrift. That's pretty cool, right? Almost magical, I'd say.

Getting started on an outline is easy, but it's not going to feel like the steps you used to take in an English classroom. For our outline creation, we are going to spoil ourselves. First we need to move away from all technology. Put your phone in another room. Turn off your computer and the TV. You can have calming music on if you'd like, but all other distractions must go.

Next, find a beautiful notebook or some sort of pad of paper that feels fresh and ready for your ideas. A nice pen is a must for this activity. Find one that is a pleasing color for you to look at. Make sure it writes easily and won't frustrate you once you get in the flow. I have a case of pens in a variety of colors that I like to use when outlining. I like my topics in one color and my subtopics in another color. Decide what works for you *before* you sit down to start writing; have all of your resources (including a glass of water) within arm's reach.

Once you have your supplies, you need to find a cozy place to write. This is the one time in the whole process of writing your book that I would steer you toward a couch, reclining chair, or something else that is both soft and supportive. I sometimes need a desk and firm chair for writing my chapters, they help me stay alert and focused, but I don't create my outline in that environment. We're going to get borderline meditative for this process and I don't want your physical discomfort to distract you from the free-flow of information you're going to be receiving.

"Tell yourself that this time is for connecting with the message of your book and that is all you will be doing."

Once you're settled with your supplies close at hand, you are going to get started organizing your thoughts. When you open to a new page in your journal or notebook, close your eyes for a few moments and take some slow, deep breaths. Clear your mind of any distractions or worries. Tell yourself that this time is for connecting with the message of your book and that is all you will be doing. Take some more deep breaths and imagine your book fully formed. You're holding it in your hand and you can feel the weight of it. When you look down at it and see its cover, what colors or feelings do you get? Does a title show up for you? Can you see your name at the top or bottom of the cover? Open your eyes and write down anything you want to remember from this brief visualization activity.

Now get into a calm state again and think about ten things you really want to convey to your reader. We may adjust this number later, but for now just stick with a goal of ten topics or subjects you definitely could explore. As you think about each topic, write it down and then skip some space and write the next topic. Do not worry about subtopics right now, unless they are vividly popping up for you. Instead, just leave some space and know that you will come back and add to them later.

*Feel free to use the simple outline below or re-create it in your journal of choice.

TABLE OF CONTENTS - 10 Things You Want to Say to Your Reader:

I. _____

_____

II._____

_____

III. _____

_____

IV. _____

_____

V._____

_____

VI. _____

_____

VII. _____

_____

VIII._____

_____

IX. _____

_____

X._____

_____

STEP 5

— ❖ —

MARK YOUR CALENDAR

In order to get through the monotony, you may feel at certain points during your book project, we are going to set up a routine. Knowing when you're going to write will help you create a "new normal" in your daily life. Having specific times to write will also raise your consciousness around your evolution as a writer. Your new role as a writer means you require time on a regular basis to... write!

I'm a big fan of early morning writing, especially under the pressure of a deadline. If I wake up with the realization that a chapter is due and I'm not done with it yet, I hop out of bed, guzzle some water, start up the coffee maker, and warm up my computer. By the time the coffee is done, I have the draft of that book open on my screen and I'm sipping and tapping away with motivation, fear, and caffeine surging through my veins. I love it!

My calendar has accountability check-ins written throughout: a writing group call (we've all got to finish ch. 3 in time!), an AM book talk with a client (everything must be sent the night before!), or a launch date (eek- I need to have the finished draft to the editor by 5pm!). I definitely feel motivated by deadlines whereas others may get seriously freaked out and potentially shut down.

Your calendar may look different than mine. You may choose to avoid high-risk deadlines that could cost you your credibility (or sanity) if the time crunch gets too compact. You can, instead, choose to write each weekday morning for 30 minutes before heading off to work. Or maybe you'll write for 2 hours each Tuesday and Thursday after dinner. You can "write" on your commute to or from work if you record your thoughts. You can send them off to be transcribed, or you can do it yourself each Wednesday while you sit on the sidelines at your daughter's karate practice. Your calendar may have specific, bi-weekly dates circled for the next chapter that needs to be completed. You could set-up a system with a coach, friend, or colleague that requires you to send your assigned writing task to them by a specific time. This semi-serious deadline might be the perfect balance between responsibility and pressure so you stay on task, but don't shut down.

A lot of us, myself included, feel some resistance to being tied to a particular day and time for writing. My only "cheat" for this step is to create *space* for writing to happen somewhat organically if you don't think you can write on demand. Creating space means setting aside time throughout your week when you could potentially write if you feel inspired. In other words, do not block out every moment of your calendar with plans, events, and obligations.

If you think you'd love to write on Sunday afternoons, for instance, don't make plans on Sunday afternoons. At all. Leave Sunday afternoons wide open so that you can leisurely stroll around the neighborhood and then sit down to your computer. If you know you work best once everyone is asleep, keep your nights open and avoid promising your spouse or yourself that you'll watch the Tonight Show.

"Create that space for a spark of creativity to catch fire and burn throughout your writing session."

One final thought: stolen moments: I get excited when my three boys settle down and watch a movie that is not tempting to me (think *Teenage Mutant Ninja Turtles*) because I know that I will have nearly two hours of uninterrupted writing time before bedtime. I feel like I'm racing against the movie to see how productive I can be. I am also guilty of dropping my kids off at our gym's childcare (free for 2 hours!) and then rushing to the neighboring coffee shop to write for 110 minutes before I have to rush back and pick them up.

Hmmm. I'm noticing a pattern in myself: I really like writing under the gun. Okay, good to know.

The other key ingredient, that is WAY more important than time, is energy. In order to be productive during your writing sessions, you need to get your vibe super high. When you think about your vibe, or vibration, think about your energy. We don't want you to be hyper, but we do want you alert and sharp. You also need to feel good. If you're fully awake and focused, but also grouchy, you may feel like your typing through a cement haze of blah. Do whatever it takes to get in a good headspace before you put fingers on keys. Take a walk, do some jumping jacks, play with your pet, dance to a song, burn some sage, meditate, try a few yoga poses, watch one (and only one) funny YouTube video, add a few exciting things to your vision board, hug someone for 30 seconds, drink some yummy tea, read a humorous book for 10 minutes, or listen to your favorite song.

Once you're in a good mood, your writing is more likely to flow.

But if it doesn't, that's okay too.

Create an environment of love and acceptance around yourself as a writer and your experience of writing. Don't allow any negative thoughts to invade your writing time. Start assuming awesomeness about yourself. Tell yourself that whatever you write today is just super. Brain dump silly ideas and keep clickety-clacking away until you get a few decent morsels. If you make a commitment to yourself to write for 30 minutes a day, then savor your beverage (authors, you *must* have a beverage) and enjoy the peace and purpose of your new writing lifestyle. Be in front of the computer, available for inspiration and insight. Know that you have a message to share and your job is to be a messenger. If the message takes its time coming out, that's a-okay. Your writing area is a judgment-free zone where you and your soon-to-be book can coexist without negativity.

Keep showing up at the scheduled time or during your organically assigned and holistically inspired space and be ready to rock and write. Put a smile on your heart some way, somehow. Then look at your WHO, WHAT, and HOW. Sit with your outline and really concentrate on one aspect of your book, like chapter 5. Really remember how you felt when you brainstormed chapter 5 on your outline. Get back to those feelings. Let them wash over you. Feel that message that bubbled up in you that day and remember the sense of urgency you felt when you scribbled down all the details you wanted to cover on that particular topic.

If you busy yourself with house-cleaning, excessive social plans, your child's Science project, or laundry (really?) then you won't have the availability inspiration needs in order to land on your fingertips. You won't be ready to write if you're off pulling weeds outside. The weeds will be gone and so will your writing time.

I love weeding, but the idea of prioritizing weeds over your writing project makes me feel blue. Your audience wants your book. Give them your book!

Review: get yourself ready to write by planning ahead and getting your vibe high.

Then start clickety-clacking away.

"Start assuming awesomeness about yourself."

What day(s) and time(s) will you set-aside during your week to write?
(Example: <u>Mondays</u> from <u>6:00am</u> to <u>7:30am</u>)

_____ from _____ to _____

_____ from _____ to _____

_____ from _____ to _____

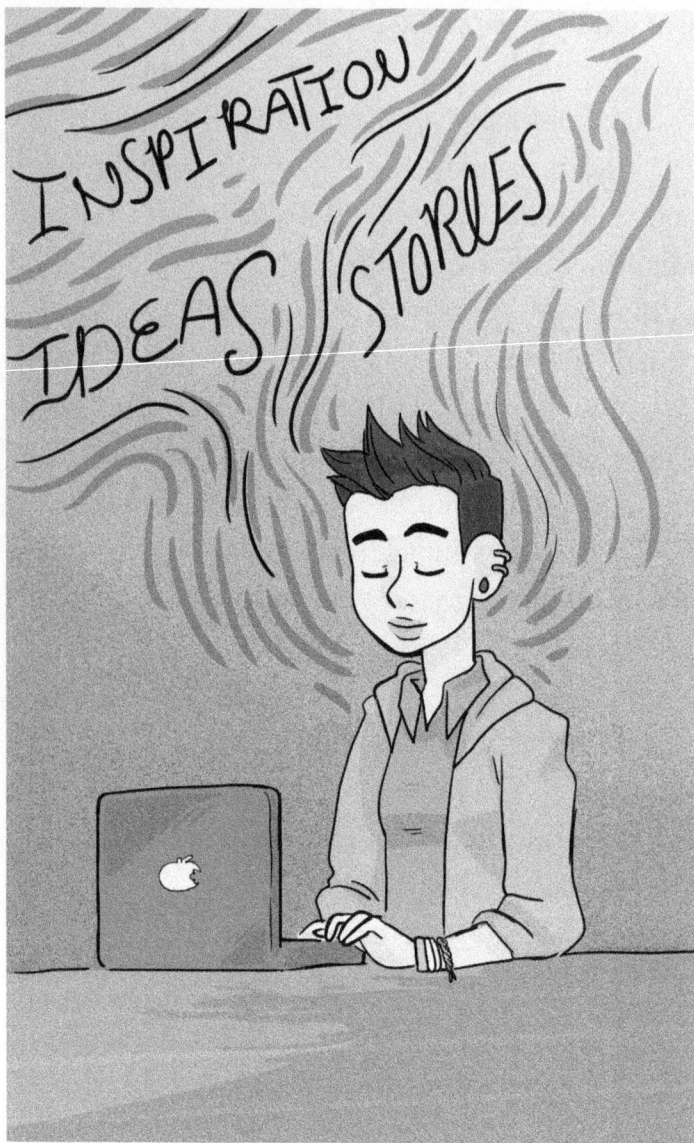

STEP 6

— ❖ —

GO DEEP INTO EACH CHAPTER

When you start the process of writing a book you must think big. It's hard for me to imagine thinking small and specific thoughts during book conception; there is no dwelling on the font or specific chapter titles. Instead, I imagine the women who will be reading my (completed?!) book and telling their friends about it. I visualize myself on stage talking with audiences who have read my book or have recently purchased it. They are holding my imaginary book in their laps, ready for me to sign it. I picture my books being discussed among thinking women and passed around to those who need to hear my friendly encouragement.

There is a temptation to stay in this "big-picture"

mindset and get all "vision board-y" about the end result of your work. I, for one, love vision boards and daydreaming. It's good floaty fun, but it's not going to get the words on the pages. At some point you have to transition from the wide-angle view to a specific microscope focus.

That time is now, friends.

We have reached the part of the writing process that involves actual writing. You've imagined, planned, organized, and scheduled. This is the clickety-clacking part of the journey I referenced. This is the time you write the words that readers are waiting to read.

Before you actually start, you can sneak a peek at your outline. See the main points you want to cover and have them at the forefront of your mind. I like to think about them as I meditate before hitting the keyboard. I close my eyes and allow the ideas to exist in my brain before they show up in the pages of my book. They can germinate for a bit and we can get comfortable with one another before I actually commit them to literary servitude.

When you read through your outline, avoid the lure of other chapters. Do not look at all of the other things you'll be covering. Don't wink at another chapter title that's particularly cute. Resist the urge to envision yourself doing some other subtopic. Do your best to stay faithful to your current chapter. Look it up and down and feel the energy that it's offering. Think about how fun it will be to take your time and really do it right. It's time to go deeper into your chapter; it's time for things to get real.

Once you type your chapter title, think about your audience. Hold their image in your mind's eye as you start a conversation with them. You want to have a consistent tone throughout your book, so briefly bring forth the voice you want to use to convey your message. It's usually enough to "see" yourself talking to them to establish the right tone, but you may still need to remind yourself of your audience from time to time. Once you get in the zone, you may lose sight of your reader if you get too enthusiastic about your message. No problem, any inconsistencies will be corrected when we revise and rewrite later!

The main goal at this point of the writing process is to get into the precious "zone" and stay there. Hopefully you are working during a period of time that you set aside to really concentrate. Once you start sharing all of the information that you have on this particular aspect of your message, you're not going to want to be interrupted. Time commitments are definitely an interruption: conference calls, appointments, pick-ups or drop-offs, meetings...all major interferences when you're on a roll with your writing.

Conversely, if you are sitting down to write for an hour, truly commit to that hour. The all-powerful "zone" likes to be respected. Therefore, if you want to get in the sacred writing zone, you need to have time set aside and actually use it! Sitting in front of the computer and typing for an hour may feel exhilarating or it may feel painful. Try not to judge yourself either way. Every writer has good and bad sessions at his or her keyboard. You don't always know how it's going to feel until you've been at it for at least 30 minutes. If your writing is not going well, do your best to stick with it and finish your time allotment with dignity. If you're in flow and the writing is going really well, considering cancelling any appointments that stand in the way of your continued progress. Either way, try to set yourself up for success!

Remember to use your calendar to create these pockets of focus and stick to them. If you write down "Draft Writing" for a two-hour block on your daily calendar, do not schedule anything else during that time. Also, do not start household chores during that time. Let key stakeholders (kids, spouses, friends) know that you will not be available during that time. Close the door or sneak off to a café and use the two hours as intended: allow yourself to get connected to your writing. You can do this!

Remember: *Do your best to stay faithful to your current chapter.*

Quick Self-Assessment:

1. Where will you be to write so you can get in the "zone" during your scheduled time?

_____

_____

_____

2. Who are the stakeholders or main characters in your real life who may interrupt your writing time?

_____   _____

_____   _____

_____   _____

_____   _____

_____   _____

_____   _____

_____   _____

3. What strategies could you use to get time for writing without interruption? (write while they watch a movie, sneak off to the library/café, get a babysitter, wait until they go to work/sleep/etc.)

_____   _____

_____   _____

_____   _____

_____   _____

_____   _____

_____   _____

_____   _____

STEP 7

---- ❖ ----

RITUALS & SELF-CARE

You are a writing workhorse. You are a writing genius. You are a writing magician.

You need to treat yourself like the amazing being that you have become. If you don't already have self-care and rituals in place for your writing sessions, let's get some now. Your writing time is a sacred space that should feel special and fulfilling. If you are writing next to a pile of laundry while children pull on you, you will have trouble remembering that you are amazing and that writing is awesome.

The first step to establishing writing rituals is to figure out what you like. The second step is to do it consistently. I, for example, like writing in the morning, in my office, in my special chair next to my sunny window. I like to hold the laptop on my lap (I'm so clever) and prop my feet up on an upholstered ottoman/table. I like silence. On the table next to me, I usually have a cup of coffee/tea, a glass of water, my planner (in case a random thought comes to mind that I must record and forget), sometimes I diffuse essential oils or burn sage. I may pick up a crystal that looks especially beautiful and have it in my pocket or on my lap. And that's it. Those are my rituals and I do them almost every time I write; like 9 out 10 times. I have trained myself to get into writing mode when these circumstances align. It feels good to enter a situation that is primed and ready for my success.

And that's it; that's the magic. I've had success writing in this setting so each time it's replicated I know on a deep, cellular level that I can do it again. I have awareness that I will open my laptop and write, feel in flow, and have a sense of accomplishment by the time my writing session is over.

I very rarely dare to mix it up anymore. I used to write everywhere and sometimes it's still fun to write while sitting in a big, cushy chair. But, in general, those options feel risky to me and I don't always want to take time to figure out how to handle the distractions that come with a new writing spot. I do not care one bit if that makes me sound lazy or boring. Having a writing ritual is one of the biggest reasons I have been able to write four books in the last few months. I have trained myself to turn it ON when I get in position with all the key elements, and I've learned how to turn it OFF when I walk out of my office and back into the mix of family life.

Quick Brainstorm: What could your writing ritual look like?

1. Describe your ideal writing environment: (room, furniture, time of day, music, smells, etc.)

_____

_____

_____

_____

_____

_____

_____

_____

_____

2. Explain what possible treats or items you will have around your workspace:

_____

_____

_____

_____

_____

_____

_____

_____

That OFF part of your writing ritual is important, too. You shouldn't feel compelled to be a writer every hour of the day. Make a conscious choice to really live life when you're not writing about it: be an independent person, be a parent, be a friend, and find a hobby or side job that excites you. Take pleasure in going on a romantic date, taking a brisk walk, running fun errands, or shopping for a treat; do things that activate other aspects of your personality. When you return to your writing ritual you will find that you crave the quiet focus of your book and you will feel satisfied that you are living life beyond your computer screen. You will have balance in your life!

Your OFF time can blend easily into your self-care regimen: no writing, just recharging. I *love* self-care stuff. Anything that I like doing or anything that gives me an energy boost falls under the category of self-care in my mind. I can entice myself to write for hours if I know I can "earn" a long walk on a beautiful day. I look forward to cups warm beverages, detox baths (baking soda, Epsom salt, essential oil), 20-minute meditations, manicures, free reading time, meeting up with friends, massages, gardening, new restaurant meals, and exercise/ sauna sessions. All of these activities are guaranteed to improve my mood and refuel me before I have to be present for a book.

Your self-care does not need to be pricey or inconvenient, but they do need to be scheduled into your life. I'm a big fan of booking classes or treatments in advance so that I will have something to look forward to *and* it will actually happen. I love knowing that I *have* to plan my day around a massage (the struggle is real). It puts a fire in me to get up and write and then "earn" that decadent break.

Look for deals online for local spas and consider a luxurious bath or rub down from your honey when you think about an in-home spa treatment. I have found wonderful (free) meditation apps on my phone and I've tried several "first-time-free" offers at new yoga center.

Self-care is often more about your mindset than it is about your budget. All of my activities would do nothing for me if I did them with an attitude of obligation. I remember going to get my nails done for the first time and seeing women looking irritable as they were getting their nails painted. Since I usually painted my own nails, I thought this was startling. Why weren't they having as much fun as I was? I vowed to always enjoy the blessing of having a manicure when someone else holds my hand and pampers me. I also told myself that if it ever got to be just another item on my to-do list, I would just go back to doing them myself at home. So far I still look forward to getting a fresh color, I think it's special to go to a salon, and I really, really like looking at my polished nails when I'm home typing.

Self-care is so important because when you ask yourself to focus on writing your first book, you are cutting into your normal lifestyle. You are adding another task to your already full plate. When you do that you are also using energy that previously went to other activities. It's almost like self-care helps you compensate for all of the demands you've put on yourself. If you take time to recharge your batteries, you will have more energy to extend to your new writing project. Often writing is not about how much time you have, but how much energy you have available to focus on the task before you. If you are feeling drained you will not be able to concentrate on your message and definitely won't be present enough to receive the wisdom that you wish to share in your story.

Another Quick Brainstorm: What are your self-care options?

_____

_____

_____

_____

_____

_____

_____

Try to fit lots of little self-care items into your day, medium ones into your week, and at least one or two big ones into your month. For me that looks like **daily** cups of tea or wine, cuddling with my husband, breathing exercises, journaling, and in-home meditating. **Weekly** I take several walks, attend group meditation sessions, go to church, watch funny movies, exercise, and read interesting things that light me up. **Monthly** I get my nails and hair done, I schedule a massage, reiki, healing touch or acupuncture appointment, I hang out with friends several times, and I go out on a date with my husband. I feel like my life is very balanced, but I understand that I set that expectation for myself and work to make sure it actually happens. I don't assume that everyone is strategic when it comes to self-care; loads of women complain that they are always feeling haggard or drained. Even men miss out and don't ever consider doing activities that will make them feel rejuvenated. We must build in these practices until they feel normal and become our status quo.

Because writing is an art and cannot be completed with the brute force one uses when cleaning a bathroom, or doing mindless office activities. Not only is concentration and stamina required, they are only the base of the process and all other skills are piled on top. You MUST have a way to replenish yourself so that you can show up to your writing with interest and energy. If you don't amp up your energy arsenal, your project will become stale and will start to feel like a burden over time.

My wish for you is that your book becomes another enjoyable aspect of your life. It would be even better if it became an energizing force on its own! You may come to see your growing book as a welcoming friend that is always eager to see you and cannot wait to hear what you have to say next. There may be a point when even the thought of your book makes you smile and you love talking about it with your friends. It's like becoming a parent: at first the idea of pregnancy sounds bizarre, strange, or wonderful, but over time you get used to the idea of bringing this new creation to life. As it grows, you grow. Eventually you are ready to take on a new reality where you are a parent and your book baby is a separate (awesome) entity. You are co-existing like rock stars together; forever.

So, set-up a routine that allows for your creativity to shine. Decide on a list of self-care options that you can sprinkle throughout your day, week, and month. And then actually follow-through with them! Remember that you *wanted* to write this book, now you have to take care of the author who can make that happen!

Writer's Oath:

I, _____, hereby swear to do what it takes to create a writing environment that will support me as an author. I also commit to self-care on a daily, weekly, and monthly basis so that I don't burn out and feel resentful towards my beautiful book baby.

_____ (your signature)

> *"You are a writing workhorse.*
> *You are a writing genius.*
> *You are a writing magician."*

STEP 8

— ❖ —

SHARE WITH YOUR PEOPLE

Becoming an author requires bravery. Beyond the bravery needed to sit in front of a computer and assume something worthwhile will pour forth, you need bravery to share that work. The act of writing is important, but allowing others to read it is even more so. I'm going to say this one more way: you must allow, ask, request, and find people to read what you wrote. Proactively seek readers out and see what they think about what you've written so far.

This could be a short chapter if that was all there was to it, but you probably already know that's not the case. Working up the nerve to ask someone to read through what you've written and then give you feedback is a multi-step process. First, you need to decide, or remember, the audience you wrote your book for in the first place. Do not ask your mother to read the latest draft of your preteen adventure book if you intended it for middle-schoolers. Seek out some actual 12 year olds and ask them to read through what you have!

Let's try a fun script:

"Hey, (nephew) Phillip! Guess what? I'm writing a book and I need some cool people to read the beginning to let me know if I'm on the right track. Could you read the first two chapters and answers a couple of questions for me?"

It's overwhelming for any reader, not just 12 year olds, to commit to reading an entire book if it's just a favor. Don't assume that everyone will be honored to be selected as a reader. Instead, consider asking them to read a chunk of your book and asking for feedback. If things go well, you can add more to your request. This sets both of you up for success, especially if you ask several readers to do the same thing.

If you ask four 7th graders at church to read two chapters, you increase the odds of getting great, diversified feedback on the beginning of your story.

If two of the preteens really like your story, you can ask them to read through two more chapters. The other two teens may not like the particular genre in which you wrote; that's okay, too. They are off the hook for reading future chapters. Look for some new readers and start them at the beginning.

This process gets you closer to "your people" or your ideal audience. Maybe you thought you wrote your book for everyone on Earth, but you didn't. You wrote your book for a special someone. They will get your jokes, marvel at your insights, and read with rapt attention. Your people are special and it's key that you recognize their specialness. As you begin to define who will be specifically drawn to your style and story, you'll also find the perfect test audience to read through your drafts. Waahoo! When you find your people and interact with them in a concrete way, you'll get valuable takeaways from their experience with your book.

Let's explore that further, what takeaways are you actually looking for as readers reflect on your work? Do you want them to tell you their thoughts on your characters? Maybe you want to know if your main character is sympathetic or if the supporting characters are realistic. If you're writing non-fiction you may want feedback on the scope of information you're presenting: too much, too little, just right? If you are still deciding on a tone or voice for your book, simply ask your readers how they felt when reading your language: too formal, too casual, just right? The more specific you get with your questioning, the better feedback you're likely to get. If you're going to invest some time in developing a professional exchange with some readers, you want to get the most out of it in order to improve your book. It is *not* helpful to have someone tell you your book is "really good" and for you to reply "thanks!" It is an ego boost and reassuring, but it doesn't give you much to go on as you plan the rest of your book or revise what you've already written.

So how do you ensure you'll get the most possible out of your readers? Try to be as structured as possible when you work with your test audience. One option is to write a list of questions (I have a sample at the end of this chapter) and send it along with the reading selection. Your readers can preview the questions and consider them *as they read* and then give you meaningful feedback afterwards. Everyone appreciates a structured assignment; when your readers agreed to help you they wanted their efforts to be productive and helpful. Help them be helpful!

Eventually, you will find that you have a steady loop of reading and feedback from your ideal audience members. If you cultivate this relationship you can also find out where they make their online purchases, how they like to learn about new things, and in what ways you can reach other readers who may enjoy your book.

Getting to know "your people" goes beyond assumptions and generalizations; actually get to know their preferences and learn to meet their needs! If you invest some time into learning about their interests and shopping habits, you are more likely to meet their needs.

Sample Questions for Readers:

1. What were your thoughts about the tone of the chapters you read? (circle all that apply)

Serious Silly Thoughtful Uplifting Depressing
Businesslike Friendly Stern Reflective Informative
Entertaining Motivating Educational Out-of-touch
Empowering

2. What aspects of ch. _ did you find confusing or
overly-complicated?
3. Would it help to have graphics, pull-quotes, or
other variations to break-up the text?
4. How did the chapters you read relate to you and
where you are in your life right now?

Remember: Becoming an author requires bravery.

STEP 9

— ❖ —

RELEASE FEARS AND SELF-SABOTAGE

There is no question that you will get really scared at some point in this journey. Even if you feel scared that you won't ever finish your book, general doubt and dismay also will visit you. Acknowledging that this is a natural part of a creative process you've never attempted before is a hugely beneficial. Just say to yourself, "I'm scared because I've never done this before and I don't know how this is going to work out."

And then keep going.

Be scared and keep going. Through the doubt and dismay, focus on the next paragraph and keep writing. Write garbage, write nonsense, write anything. When you keep going, you are messaging to your ego, your fear-center, that you will not be deterred. Even when you miss days or weeks of writing because it's easier to go return to living life as usual instead of living life as a part-time writer, go back to the computer. Physically put yourself in front of screen and pick-up where you left off.

A really big part of me wants to tell you to meditate, journal, run around the block, have sex, go on a vacation, get a massage, or brew the perfect cup of tea. I want to tell you something peaceful and calming, but I KNOW that will only lead to further procrastination. Instead of delaying, let's skip to the true solution, which is to find peace IN THE WRITING ITSELF.

Returning to your friend, your book, you can heal the pain that comes from fear. Your worries about being read, understood, embarrassed, or ignored by readers is not real. You're living a self-created nightmare when you embrace the self-doubt that comes in the middle of a project. You are allowed to reject that mentality, but you're also allowed to believe it.

Because the choice is yours, I want you get

back to writing to see if your opinion of yourself changes. Often when we return to a message that we feel passionately about, we are reminded of our purpose. In the act of typing again, we feel a connection to our future audience. Writing itself calms our fears and puts them in perspective: doing new things, daring different projects will always trigger uncertainties. Our mind, or ego, wants to keep us safe and when we venture out to new spaces and places it kind of freaks out. As long as you know that's part of the role the ego plays, you can listen to its warning without stopping. Understand that your first book will probably not be as good as your second book (thanks for telling me, ego!) but then listen to your heart or gut. That voice will lovingly remind you that in order to actually get to book #2 you have to write book #1!

So now we are back to our straightforward, "keep going" mentality. We plug away at our book by typing letters on the page and watching the pages fill. We smile at the edits that will soon come. We wonder how much of what we type now will end up in the final version of our first published work. We keep typing.

It doesn't matter at this point if we will succeed or fail in the future. We are staying present in this moment of effort and creating. We are making something that has never existed before and we are enjoying our role as a creator. The power that comes through us is unique to this space and time. We hold more power now than we will in any post-production activity. Our words are the content that any future success will rely on.

What you are writing each time you sit in front of the computer should be peacefully shared, not fearfully extracted. Staying at the keyboard will probably take you through a range of emotions that aren't all positive, but you can choose to give focus to the productive, high-energy feelings you have when you think about why you were initially called write your first book.

Think about why you bothered to write: did you have a story to share? Are you sharing your experiences so that others will be able to find happiness and independence? Do you want readers to reflect, learn, and grow? Is your book about entertaining readers so that they can escape from reality for a short while? Regardless of your reason, you can choose to connect with your original purpose every time you sit down to write.

If there is meditation in writing, it's in knowing that you are not an awesome individual who has great writing skills, but that you are a conduit, a channel, for a message that is bigger than you. The meditation, or soul connection, during writing comes when you understand that your book is bigger than you in ways you cannot understand. You don't need to know who will actually read your book, you don't need to understand what will happen to your life once you publish it and step into the role of author. You don't even need to believe that anything will happen at this point. Your only job is to share the message you feel called to share. That's it! Just keep doing that without excuses.

When you are done sharing every aspect of the message that has come to you, *then* you can worry about will happen next. There will be a huge shift in focus when you have to choose a book cover, write a blurb for the back cover, or market your book to potential readers. But that's not what is happening now. For now, you push "pause" on apprehension and slide into the cozy space that is full of possibility, creativity, and fun.

Your book is fun! Writing it is an expression of universal wisdom coming through YOU! You are the super lucky person who gets to share this particular topic with whoever is lucky enough to read it!

Releasing fear and self-sabotage is less about fighting the negativity that can creep in, and is more about side-stepping those pitfalls and staying on the path before you. As you continue on your writing journey, whether with this book or future writings, it's critical to remember that those writing roadblocks do not mean you should stop. They are reminders that you have gone off your usual path. They are warnings from a part of you that wants you to always play it safe and never take risks. You will need to continue to recognize these bumps without being thrown off your path. Slide to the left, duck to the right. See the doubt and smile at yourself. Thank the doubt for caring enough to show up while you're in the middle of this new project. Pat it on the back or even give your feelings of doubt a big hug. Then go on your way without excuses or delay.

When you recognize the feelings that de-plete you *before* they turn into mammoth forms of self-sabotage, procrastination, or complete creative paralysis, you are better able to stay in flow with your writing. There is no need to say, "I'm not afraid of failure." You are allowed to, instead, be honest and say, "I'm afraid of failure, but I want to keep trying anyway." You're acknowledging your ego's warnings (ie. failure is a possibility) while diffusing the devastating impact that you perceive a failure might have. In other words: don't deny your fears, work around and through them. See your fears and decide not to be defined by them.

Self-sabotage comes when you help your fears halt your joy. It feels bad to see your joy slip away, but it's strangely comfortable and empowering be-cause you are the one doing the damage. We can all justify our actions, and self-sabotage is no dif-ferent. I have seen writers do this with precision and stealth. They will confidently tell me why they cannot continue writing and may even become out-raged if someone challenges that notion. You *had* to take the dog on a walk, you *had* to pick-up the dry-cleaning, you *had* to empty the dishwasher.

All these tasks had to be completed during your book writing time. Darn those errands! If only you weren't so busy.

The self-sabotage that shows up when writing a book is extremely practical. It tells you that it's not worth your time or money to write a book. It seems like this comes up for first-time authors more than other areas of expression. Does that same voice show up for people who love to knit and spend time and money on that art? Do cyclists and runners fret about the financial payoff of their efforts? How about folks who love camping and find connection with the outdoors- do they worry about whether they will be a failure? What if we thought about writing as something we love to do that lights us up? What if writing was an activity like knitting, biking, running, or camping- something we do because we feel called to do it?

Given some perspective, I think we can release some of the worry we carry around if we remember that book writing is just another thing we can do for pleasure. Like exercising, writing might alleviate stress and free you from painful memories in the past. After relieving yourself from those burdens, you will be more open to pleasure. Like painting or photography, your writing might be a form of artwork that can last through generations. Like volunteering, your book may give back to people that desperately need love and attention. Even though you may not have thought about your published writing being like scrapbooking, you are weaving together elements of yourself in a way a similar way. Future generations, and loved ones now, will be able to share your thoughts in an easy package. Your book is a collection of your memories that are polished and permanent in their presentation, it's pretty cool.

So let's reflect on YOU specifically. What might stand in the way of your completed book? Please reflect honestly below and stay open to the ways your "practical" and "reasonable" excuses may be blocking your beautiful book from coming into existence.

Reflections on Self-Sabotage:

1. When you feel overwhelmed or negative about your book, what are the reasons you attach to your

feelings (examples: too much other work, writing isn't good enough, no one will read this, I'll embarrass my family, more important/interesting projects, etc.)

_____

_____

_____

_____

_____

_____

2. What hobbies or activities do you enjoy that also take time, energy, and possibly funds? (examples: reading, shopping, landscaping, fitness, travel, decorating, church, schooling, etc.)

_____

_____

_____

_____

_____

_____

3. What do you do when you don't want to write?

_____

_____

_____

_____

_____

_____

_____

4. In general, how do you feel when you *do* write?

_____

5. How do you feel when you do NOT write (and you know you could)? _____

"Your only job is to share the message you are called to share."

STEP 10

— ❖ —

RE-READ IT ALL

nd then one day...you're done. You've written an entire book. You finally reached the end of your detailed outline and you've covered all of your chapters. You are finished!

Haha, I laugh at your celebration. You are NOT done. Congratulations on finishing your first draft, but don't get too jazzed about walking away from your book.

At this point you are definitely not done working on your manuscript. Now you enter the stage of writing that will transform your book and make it a cohesive, polished product. You must re-read it all. From start to finish: read, read, read.

I like to sit down from early morning until late

evening to read straight through. This concept of simply "reading" is a bit of a fallacy since you will hardly be reading the entire time. Instead, you will read two sentences and see a spelling error that you can quickly fix. Then you'll read a paragraph and realize you used the word "strategy" four times. Then you'll notice that you changed a character's name midway through a page. Corrections jump out left and right like eager children who want free candy. They pop up and enthusiastically take whatever you'll give them. I learn I need to give out more commas and cut back on all the semi-colons; I love semi-colons. I notice all of the you're/your errors and I make sure that things stay consistently in past or present tense. I fret over repeated words and think of synonymous phrases for "she became keenly aware" and words like "slid".

I never notice these repeated words as I write the first time since I don't go back and re-read every chapter as I write. Why not? I don't want to get bogged down in style/grammar stuff while I'm in the middle of the story-telling. Whether it's fiction or non-fiction, erotica, or self-help, I want to move *forward* with the message I'm sharing. I am not worried about going back to what I wrote 45 minutes ago to see if I like it. It's fine, I got it out of me and it's going to stay on the page for the time being. I want to keep moving in the direction of the finish line so that the energy of the message stays high. When I work with new writers who go back again and again to analyze the one or two chapters they've written, I wince. They work and rework the beginning of a book that hasn't even hit its groove yet. Those chapters may get cut, or they may get reworked or shifted to another part of the story. I know that my job is to get all of the information out in a fluid, easy, connected way. I stay in flow and high vibe while I write. I don't judge myself and I don't criticize my writing at that time.

When I'm in the writing or producing stage, I just let it all out. When I finish that process, I take a break. Like walk away for a day or week. Forget about writing. Do something that isn't related to writing. You can focus on other aspects of your book like the cover or general promotion or your launch, but don't go back to read it right after you finish.

After you and your book have some time to miss

one another, set aside a huge chunk of time: a day, two days, maybe even a week, and have a grand reunion. You two will connect on a different level. You will suddenly see that this writing is yours, but it's not yours. It seems vaguely familiar, but also new and fresh. You can proofread your own writing with a relaxed perspective while still knowing how you want it to look all together. When you revise your book in this way, you easily see the big picture. Your message should be consistent, but so should your organization, voice, and rhythm. It's hard to pick up on those overarching characteristics if you're always editing the same day or soon thereafter.

Walking away also makes it more fun! You get to experience your book (kind of) like an actual first-time reader. Especially if you're like me; I can never remember what I wrote. It's definitely a blessing/curse quality of mine: I enjoy reading it without a lot of recognition, but it can be disorienting not to remember writing something. In the end, it's great for the revision stage since I don't feel very connected to the details of the writing. Instead, I can edit my work in the same way I edit a stranger's work. It's all very systematic and rarely emotional.

Asking your beta readers to review your book right after *you* proofread and edit it will help get your book to the final, polished stage quickly. Anytime you can overlap work on your book, you will maximize your efficiency. Send out the entire book with the note that you need a turn-around time of 1 week. Explain what you're looking for from their edits: feedback on content, an eye for grammar or spelling mistakes, areas you could provide more clarity, etc. If you're sending the draft to your readers digitally, make sure you include a brief email portion thanking them for their time, telling them what you'd like them to look for, and when you need their notes. If you only want them to read for flow and clarity, say that. Be as specific as possible so your readers will feel confident giving you their candid thoughts. Many times we need to be given permission to be really honest with others. When you give your readers that permission, you're more likely to get really good reflections on your book.

List 3-5 people you could ask to read your edited draft, the first draft *after* you read and revise.

1. _____
2. _____
3. _____
4. _____
5. _____

What 3-5 areas would you like them to focus on as they read? (grammar/spelling, content, clarity, character development, sentence and word variety, etc.)

1. _____
2. _____
3. _____
4. _____
5. _____

Remember: *Be as specific as possible so your readers will feel confident giving you their candid thoughts.*

Once you send out your email with the version you'd like to have reviewed, step back and allow your readers to have some space. Try to avoid any follow-up emails until the day before the comments are due. Send a courtesy reminder email that you'll need all responses by midnight the next day so that you can make needed changes before you send your draft to an editor. Don't be surprised if you don't get everyone's responses by the deadline. While your book is a priority to you, for many other people, it's just one more thing on their to-do list. If you have stragglers, follow-up the day after the due date with one last email asking if they have thoughts for you before you send your work off to a professional. If they respond, great, if they don't reply, move on.

The final step in this process is the professional edit. You can be an English teacher and an excellent writer and I'd still recommend sending your work to a professional editor. You can find an editor online or you may receive those services from a publisher you're working with. Regardless, they are critical because they will catch mistakes that you and your beta readers overlooked. You will then be more relaxed knowing that you have fixed all errors before your book goes to print. It's a pretty terrible experience to read through your published book only to see a misspelled word. Save yourself that agony!

It should be noted that you can also ask your editor to focus on specific aspects of your book. In fact, you can hire a **line editor** who focuses on grammar, spelling, syntax, and overall structure or you can work with a **content editor** who mostly focuses on your story, its clarity, and cohesion.

STEP 11

———— ❖ ————

STEP INTO YOUR PURPOSE

When your book is done, *you* are just beginning. Beyond the publishing and promotion of your new book, things have shifted. In short, you are different after writing a book. In general, you are lighter than before you began. After putting so much onto the page, you can move forward with an ease and flow that was not previously available to you. All of your painful experiences, deep insights, clever stories, or witty observations can live within the sacred space of your book. They no longer need to be stored in your brain taking time and energy away from your focus on either the present moment or other, future, endeavors.

You have relinquished some responsibility because you have decided not to carry those stories around anymore. By investing the time and effort into writing them down, you gave yourself the freedom to move forward with your life.

In that moving forward, however, you will notice new and different responsibilities appear. Suddenly others will look to you as a role-model for self-determination and persistence. They will see you as a success simply for finishing something that you started. In our modern culture that values quick and disposable foods, actions, and ideas, you are stepping into a different category when you slow things down to contemplate and synthesize concepts.

In addition to the mere act of completing a project, you will notice that people around you, even those who don't read your book, will assume that you are an expert on the subject area of your book. Do not shy away from your role as an authority. Continue to learn more and more about your topic and embrace this new aspect of your identity. Just like when you were writing, remember that you must keep going even when you are uncomfortable. Being seen as a writer or an author may feel awkward at first, but remember that you were open to this evolution when you committed to writing. You didn't spend all of those hours working on your book so that life could stay the same; no, you wanted to live a bigger life with new experiences!

Now is the time to step into your purpose and notice how others need you in their lives. Are they looking to you to guide them, inspire them, inform them? If you are able to help others in some way, don't hesitate, do it! If you are asked to speak on your book's subject matter, go for it! When people try to get you to share your wisdom, do not negate your power or their opinion of you by dismissing them. Step into your new role. Learn how to feel comfortable traversing the world in a new way.

This is not to say that everyone will instantly love you and adore your first book. Accept any feedback you may receive and make changes if needed. Listen to the words that people say to you, but also stay aware of the energy with which they say them. Notice when others are excited for you and your brave step into the unknown. Sometimes the feedback you get is admiration because you actually took a risk and did something many other people are scared to do. Reflect that excitement back to those around you and encourage them to take the next step towards their secret ambitions. Stay present and hold the space for those who seem to suddenly be attracted to you. These are new members of your tribe. They are the ones who are bold enough to introduce themselves. Many others will watch you and your actions from afar. They're not creepy; they're shy. Your tribe will continue to grow as long as you continue to share your message.

Embrace the conversations that will come and confidently step into your purpose. Your first book is just the beginning of the shift that will transform your life.

You wanted this; now own it.

ABOUT THE AUTHOR

❖

Amy R Brooks loves working with first-time authors. She knows that given time and permission, most people can grow and heal through sharing their wisdom through writing.

She renews her peace and her energy on a daily basis in her Maryland home that she shares with three silly sons, two snuggly cats, and one sensational husband.

Find out how you can work with Amy as a speaker or a coach.

AmyRBrooks.com

Facebook: *Amy Brooks: Author, Speaker & Writing Coach*

Instagram: *AmyReneeBrooks*

Twitter: *@amyreneebrooks*

Are you ready to work with a (super) illustrator and graphic designer? Contact Abe Kane immediately!

She will rock the socks off your project!

www.abekane.com

abekanedesign@gmail.com

She will rock the socks off your project